MW01286738

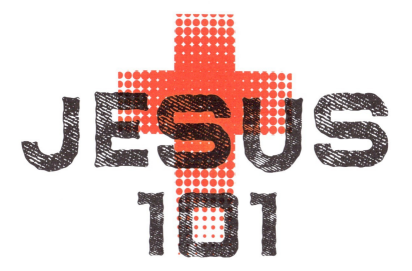

JESUS 101

30 DEVOTIONS ON GETTING
TO KNOW THE SAVIOR

Be courageous!
Joshua 1:9

Mrs. Rose

No part of this work may be reproduced or transmitted in any form or by any means, electronic or mechanical, including photocopying and recording, or by any information storage or retrieval system, except as may be expressly permitted in writing by the publisher. Requests for permission should be addressed in writing to Lifeway Press®, 200 Powell Place, Suite 100, Brentwood, TN 37027-7514.

ISBN 978-1-0877-4797-2
Item 005833364
Dewey Decimal Classification Number: 242
Subject Heading: DEVOTIONAL LITERATURE / BIBLE STUDY AND TEACHING / GOD

Printed in the United States of America

Student Ministry Publishing
Lifeway Resources
200 Powell Place, Suite 100
Brentwood, TN 37027-7514

We believe that the Bible has God for its author; salvation for its end; and truth, without any mixture of error, for its matter and that all Scripture is totally true and trustworthy. To review Lifeway's doctrinal guideline, please visit www.lifeway.com/doctrinalguideline.

Unless otherwise noted, all Scripture quotations are taken from the Christian Standard Bible®, Copyright © 2017 by Holman Bible Publishers. Used by permission. Christian Standard Bible® and CSB® are federally registered trademarks of Holman Bible Publishers.

publishing team

Director, Student Ministry
Ben Trueblood

Manager, Student Ministry Publishing
John Paul Basham

Editorial Team Leader
Karen Daniel

Writer
Nikki Tigg

Content Editor
Kyle Wiltshire

Production Editor
Brooke Hill

Graphic Designer
Jon Rodda

TABLE OF CONTENTS

INTRO

Do you remember your first day of kindergarten? You may not recall much about it, but one thing is for sure—you know a lot more today than you did on that day. No one walks into school knowing everything. Everyone has to learn the basics and build upon that knowledge to understand more complex subjects.

The same is true when it comes to your faith in Jesus. You might have been going to church for as long as you can remember, and you might know all the "classic" stories of the Bible. The truth is, you have a lot more to learn. You have a lot more lessons to apply to your life. Guess what? You're not alone. Everyone who walks the earth today is in the same boat. We all are works in progress, growing in our knowledge and understanding of who Jesus is.

That's why this book is titled Jesus 101. The 100 level courses in school are usually the foundational ones that everything else is built upon. When it comes to our faith, there are some basic, really important things we need to know first. Jesus is at the top of that list.

More importantly than knowledge, this book is about moving the information you have about Jesus in your head, to your heart. Having a bunch of knowledge about Jesus might help you win a trivia contest, but it won't do you much good unless it guides you to know Him personally. He has to change your heart because your heart leads you. If the life and teachings of Jesus have made their way into your heart through a relationship with Him, you are more inclined to live in a way that reflects who He is and who He's leading you to be.

This book walks through His whole life, from birth to ascension and everywhere in between. If you have just become a follower of Jesus, these next thirty days will give you a great foundation to build on. If you've walked with Jesus for years, these devotions will help cement what you believe and challenge you to share this good news with others.

Welcome to Jesus 101. A life changing experience awaits!

GETTING STARTED

This devotional contains 30 days of content, broken down into sections. Each day is divided into three elements—discover, delight, and display—to help you answer core questions related to Scripture.

discover |

This section helps you examine the passage in light of who God is and determine what it says about your identity in relationship to Him. Included here is the daily Scripture reading, focus passage, along with illustrations and commentary to guide you as you explore God's Word.

delight |

In this section, you'll be challenged by questions and activities that help you see how God is alive and active in every detail of His Word and your life. We've given you a whole page to write your answers to these questions, so really think and dig in.

display |

Here's where you take action. Display calls you to apply what you've learned through each day's devotion.

> **Each day also includes a prayer activity at the conclusion of the devotion.**

Throughout the devotional, you'll also find other resources to help you connect with the topic, such as Scripture memory verses, additional resources, and articles that help you go deeper into God's Word.

IN THE BEGINNING

Jesus has always been. However, His time on earth had a definite beginning. These first eight days chronicle the beginning of Jesus's life here in our world. Try to imagine that; God in the flesh, having to learn all the things we have learned—like how to walk, talk, and make friends. As God, He's completely different from us, but as a person, He's just like us. That's a comforting thought. Our Savior understands what it feels like to be human.

THE LIGHT OF JESUS

discover |

READ JOHN 1:1-18.

The Word became flesh and dwelt among us. We observed his glory, the glory as the one and only Son from the Father, full of grace and truth.
—John 1:14

Our human brains can sometimes have a hard time comprehending that Jesus, God in the flesh, is so powerful that He's always existed and that He loves us so much that He came to rescue us from darkness. He left His perfect home in heaven so that we might know His light.

Jesus has always existed, but not long after humans were created, sin entered the world. As humans, we are sinful by nature, which is a problem because sin separates us from God. But Jesus is our solution because He never sinned. He left heaven, put on flesh, and came to earth to heal our broken relationship with God. He is full of grace and truth—His truth is the light for our lives.

The world you live in is dark, and until you receive the light of Jesus, your heart is dark, too. He came to earth to dwell among us and in us. After saying yes to Jesus, His light begins to shine in your heart. It is only His light that makes a difference in your life. You, in your own effort, can't drive out darkness; you must rely on the light that comes from Jesus.

He came to dwell on earth so that He could dwell within you, so allow His presence in your heart to shine bright!

delight |

How does the reality of Jesus change a dark heart?

How have you seen Jesus's light working in the lives of others?

display

Turn off all lights or go into a dark room. Think about how the smallest light would illuminate the area. That dark room is a picture of our hearts without Jesus. Darkness represents sin, but Jesus came to rescue you from darkness and offers you the opportunity to live in the light.

Google a picture of sunshine and make it your screensaver for the day. Every time you look at your phone today, be reminded that Jesus's light is shining in your heart.

If you are hiding the light that Jesus gave you, write down one thing you can do today to shine brighter.

Spend a moment thanking God for his grace, truth, love, and light. Thank Him for sending Jesus to dwell among us and thank Him for the love shown to you by sending Jesus into your life. Ask Him to help you operate in His light and to point others to Him. Have a moment of silence and ask Him to show you ways you can let your light shine even brighter today. Remember what it felt like before you experienced Jesus's light and pray for those who haven't accepted Jesus into their lives. If there is darkness in your heart because you haven't accepted Him, invite Him to come into your life so that His light will shine brightly within you.

DAY 2

TEEN MOM

discover |

READ LUKE 1:26-38.

*Now listen: You will conceive and give birth to
a son, and you will name him Jesus.*
—Luke 1:31

God sending Jesus into the world was a big deal! We'd expect Him to use a wise, wealthy, older woman to be His mother; instead, He used a teenager. What was so special about her?

God saw that Mary was humble, available, and faithful to Him. Despite her age, He used her to perform the greatest miracle ever—the miracle of conceiving and giving birth to Jesus! The presence of Jesus in our lives changes everything. Without Jesus, our relationship with God would be broken with no hope of being repaired. Jesus's arrival on earth was the first step in God's amazing plan of redemption—and He put His plan in motion using a teenager.

God showed His faithfulness by sending His Son from heaven to earth, just as He promised. Mary showed her faithfulness by being obedient to listen and trust God's plan. Despite your home life, amount of money, age, or amount of followers you have on social media, God can use you for His plan. You can impact this world!

Don't make the mistake of thinking that you're unable to be used by God because you're a teenager. God trusted a teen to be Jesus's mom. God used Mary to change our world, and He can use your faithfulness to change the world as well.

delight |

Mary was confused, shocked, and had questions about what the angel was telling her. Have you ever felt that? How does Mary's story encourage you?

Mary showed herself to be faithful, and it changed the world. How do you see your faithfulness impacting others?

display |

Read the key verse. First, Mary was told to listen, then she was told what was going to happen and was given further directions. God used her faithfulness, but first, she had to listen, and then obey. Set a timer on your phone or watch for two minutes to spend in silence to listen to God.

Describe how you feel God leading you.

How do you plan to respond in obedience today?

Take a moment to think about God and praise Him for being ever-present, holy, unchanging, and for His divine nature. Thank Him for His plan to send Jesus to earth to be a Savior for all who accept Him and for the boldness you can have as a teen to know that you can be used for His Kingdom. Admit to God when you've let your age or lack of obedience limit your kingdom activity. Pray for other students who may struggle in this area. Ask God to increase your desire to listen to His voice and obey His Word.

DAY 3

FOR ALL PEOPLE

discover |

READ LUKE 2:1-20.

Then she gave birth to her firstborn son, and she wrapped him tightly in cloth
and laid him in a manger, because there was no guest room available for them.
—Luke 2:7

Hundreds of years before Jesus was born, the Jews were expecting a king. They had been expecting the arrival of this great king for over eight hundred years! They knew this king would be a savior—the Messiah. But their expectation for the arrival of this king and the reality of how He came into the world were two different things. They expected for their king to be born under royal conditions and for the highest officials to know about his birth first; but this King's arrival was a humble one.

You probably don't know anyone that was born in a stable—but Jesus was! Mary gave birth in the presence of animals and had to place her newborn baby in a feeding trough. What a humble way for a king to be born! Even though Jesus was born in that type of setting, it didn't limit His purpose. It actually points to His purpose. He was born not only to save the wealthy and powerful, but He was born for all people—no matter their class.

We see this by who the angels told first about His birth. The shepherds were a lower class of people who had no political power or wealth. But God chose to reveal the one and only long awaited Messiah, the King of kings, the Light of the world, to ordinary men working outside in a field. God shows us that Jesus is for all people, and no one is excluded.

delight |

If God doesn't look down on people who aren't wealthy, why do you think people in our world today do?

Think about the reality that Jesus was sent from heaven to be born for you—no matter your popularity, amount of money your family has, or your GPA. How does this truth make you feel?

display

When Jesus was born, there was no room for Him in the lodging place. His presence on earth changes everything, and we must make room for His presence. As believers, we often say yes to Jesus, but don't invite His presence into our daily lives and decisions.

What are two things you can do today to make room for Jesus in your life?

Praise God for His great love toward all people, His perfect plan, and His faithfulness. Ask for forgiveness if you have treated people poorly or excluded them based on their material possessions or popularity. Ask God to help you forgive others who may have treated you poorly based on your differences.

Thank God for sending Jesus for all people and not excluding anyone. Thank Him for the gift of Jesus coming to earth to be a Savior for your sinfulness. Pray for God to increase your love for others and to show you who in your life needs to hear about the good news of Jesus.

DAY 4
JUST LIKE YOU

READ LUKE 2:41-52.

*And Jesus increased in wisdom and stature, and
in favor with God and with people.*
—Luke 2:52

What do you picture when you think of Jesus? A baby in the manger? Him on the Cross? Healing people? How often do you think of Him as a middle schooler? We tend to forget this stage of His life, but Jesus was just like us. He had parents to obey, chores to do, and friends He wanted to hang out with. He had to grow up as a normal kid just like you do; the big difference is that He never sinned. He knew He was placed on earth to fulfill God's purpose and, eventually, He sinlessly completed His job.

Although He was fully God in flesh, He had to grow and mature as a human teen boy. As He grew older, everything increased—His favor, wisdom, and even His height. Remember, He was only a twelve-year-old at this point in the story. The same Jesus who died for your sins on the cross can relate to you as a teen because He was one as well.

You can be comforted knowing that Jesus knows how it feels to grow up through all the stages that you are going through or have experienced. You may have gone through issues as a middle or high schooler and thought Jesus couldn't relate to your situation. However, Jesus was fully human and went through adolescent and teen years, and He fully understands exactly how you feel as you face teen issues. He had to grow physically, emotionally, and spiritually, just like you do.

delight |

What are two of your favorite childhood memories?

Imagine Jesus being the same age as you and right there with you. How does this help you realize that He was your age and can relate to everything about you?

display

Jesus didn't take shortcuts during His life on earth. He had to mature physically, intellectually, and socially, just like the rest of us. He also increased in favor with God—He experienced spiritual growth.

What are two things you need to do to grow spiritually?

Physical growth is great. Being smart is great, too, but growing spiritually is what will change your life. Make a plan to implement both things from above into your life for the next thirty days. Just imagine how, like Jesus, you will grow in favor with God!

Praise Jesus for being obedient and staying on course even as a twelve-year-old boy. Because He lived as a teen, thank Him for the reality that He can understand your hurts, pains, relationship struggles, and life as a teen. Ask Him to help you remember that He can relate to your situation because He had to grow up through the teen years just like you. Ask for an increased awareness of His ability to understand and relate to every situation you face. Pray to grow as He did. Pray for increased wisdom, stature, and favor with God and with people.

THE WORD

became flesh

and dwelt

among us.

We observed his glory, the glory as the one and only Son from the Father, full of **GRACE&TRUTH.**

DAY 5

IN ALL THINGS

discover |

READ MATTHEW 3:13-17.

*And a voice from heaven said, "This is my beloved
Son, with whom I am well-pleased."
—Matthew 3:17*

As Christians, we need to be baptized because it is a public celebration of moving from death to life through our faith in Jesus. It symbolizes the change in our hearts and the old sinful self becoming new.

It's easy to see why baptism is important for us, but why was it important for Jesus to be baptized? His cousin, John, who was known for baptizing others, wondered the same thing. John realized he was a sinful person who had to repent and needed baptism, but he questioned why Jesus needed to be baptized. Jesus answered him, "this is the way for us to fulfill all righteousness" (Matt. 3:15).

Jesus was baptized, but because He was sinless, He didn't need a change in His heart. However, He went through with baptism to be obedient to God and to be an example for us. Jesus always completes the will of His Father. It was important to Him to be obedient and fulfill all righteousness. God was pleased with His actions, as we can tell from the key verse. God was heard audibly speaking from heaven. He was speaking about Jesus, but He directed His words to the people who were present. He shared His approval for His beloved Son and honored Him in front of others.

God desires obedience. He desired it from Jesus and He desires it from us—not only in baptism, but in all things.

delight

It was important to Jesus to be obedient. Is obedience to God important to you? How is your answer made evident in your life?

Are there times when it is hard for you to be obedient? How do you respond in those times?

display |

Jesus is perfect, but we are not. An imperfection we sometimes have is struggling to be obedient. Jesus was never disobedient because His heart found joy in pleasing His Father.

What are three things you find pleasure in?

1.

2.

3.

Do any of these cause you to be disobedient?

Read John 14:23. What is obedience linked to?

When our love for Jesus grows, so does our obedience. Jesus obeyed God because of His love for Him.

> **Thank Jesus for being the perfect example for us by being obedient in all things, down to the last detail. Ask Him to grow your love for Him and to desire to be obedient even when it's hard. Pray for the courage to say no to temptation and live a life submitted to God. Confess the times you've been disobedient and share with Him why you may be struggling in certain areas. Pray for your friends who are wrestling with disobedience. Pray that their hearts will desire goodness and righteousness.**

DAY 6
OUR GO-TO

discover |

READ MATTHEW 4:1-11.

Then Jesus told him, "Go away, Satan! For it is written:
Worship the Lord your God, and serve only him."
—Matthew 4:10

Unfortunately, temptation is a part of life. As a teen, you may be tempted to lie to your parents, break rules at home or school, or do wrong things in order to gain popularity. Temptation will always be a part of your life, but the key is knowing how to handle it.

God's Word is our guide to navigate life—it is 100% true and can be trusted. We look to it for direction on how to handle tough things in life like temptation. Jesus is our example. When He was in the wilderness being tempted, He used Scripture to overcome it. He can relate to how you feel when you struggle with temptation because He faced it, too. He teaches us an important lesson as we face temptation: Jesus didn't rely on His feelings or circumstances; He relied on God's Word. We see how powerful Scripture is because it is the very tool Jesus used when He was tempted by Satan.

Jesus shows us the importance of making sure God's Word is our go-to source for help in hard times. Read Matthew 4:4—Jesus made it clear that we are to rely on Scripture as we live our daily lives. It is hard to rely on Scripture if you don't read it or have any memorized. Make a practice of reading and memorizing Scripture so that you can fight temptation the way Jesus modeled for you.

delight |

Do you ever wonder if Jesus can really relate to the temptations you face? How does today's reading encourage you?

Are you tempted the most when you are alone or with friends? What can you begin doing to help you win the battle against temptation?

display

Each time Jesus was tempted, not only did He quote Scripture, but He mentioned God each time. He always pointed back to the Father.

On a separate piece of paper, write down the three verses in which Jesus used Scripture and mentioned God the Father to resist Satan. Say each verse aloud and keep the paper with you to help you fight temptation today.

Read Hebrews 4:15. Add this verse to your paper. Read all four verses three times throughout your day today.

> Thank God for the examples in Scripture that help you understand how to deal with temptation. Thank Him for the comfort in knowing that Jesus walked through temptation and can sympathize with you and help you as you face it. Confess any areas of unconfessed sin where you have given in to temptation and ask Him to help you model Jesus's actions the next time you face temptation. Ask God to help you worship and serve Him above all else. Spend time thanking Him for His love, greatness, and compassion, reminding yourself that He is worthy of your worship and praise.

DAY 7

"FOLLOW ME"

discover |

READ LUKE 5:1-11.

When Simon Peter saw this, he fell at Jesus's knees and said, "Go away from me, because I'm a sinful man, Lord!"
—Luke 5:8

When Jesus started His ministry, He chose to be surrounded by ordinary disciples who became His friends. Those who were chosen left everything to follow Him. Like the disciples, we are ordinary people, and we have the same choice to make—to leave what's comfortable and accept the invitation to follow Jesus. Following Jesus means we accept He is in the lead and we are not. Like Peter, it means understanding that we are sinful and He is so much greater and worthy of our worship.

When Peter heard Jesus teaching and witnessed His power for himself, he realized Jesus was holy and realized his own sinfulness. Yet Jesus still invited him to be His disciple, and He invites us as well. Immediately, Peter, James, and John left everything and followed Jesus. They left behind the life that was comfortable—not to mention the ton of fish they just caught—to follow Him. The fish they caught could have made them a lot of money, but they abandoned their catch to follow Jesus.

You probably aren't a fisherman like these guys, but you likely have made changes in your life since following Jesus. When we accept Jesus, we accept where He leads us. He's the leader, and we are to follow Him alone. We leave behind the worldly activities, habits, and possibly even money (as the disciples did) as we follow Jesus.

delight |

How has following Jesus cost you?

How does knowing Jesus invited ordinary people like the fishermen in the story encourage you as you follow Him?

display |

Movies, TV, and social media tell you that you need to be a celebrity or an influencer to make an impact. These days, you have so much pressure to be famous, to be noticed, and to be different in order to gain approval and get followers.

The world tells you to do more or be more, but Jesus wants and loves you just the way you are. He desires you no matter how many friends or followers you have. He is asking you to follow Him, just like He asked His ordinary disciples.

Jesus uses ordinary people. Write down three ordinary things about yourself. Beside that, write down how Jesus can use these ordinary things about you.

Spend time thanking Jesus for His love for all people and the invitation to follow Him no matter the education level, income, or country you live in. Thank Him for the privilege of being called His follower. Confess any times you haven't spoken up or lived boldly because you felt too ordinary or because you desired worldly things. Confess any sin that is keeping you from following Jesus completely. Ask Jesus to help you boldly follow Him despite the pressures from the world. Pray for any friends who may be following the crowd and not Jesus.

DAY 8
IT'S A MIRACLE!

discover |

READ JOHN 2:1-11.

*Jesus did this, the first of his signs, in Cana of Galilee. He
revealed his glory, and his disciples believed in him.*
—John 2:11

Jesus's ministry was filled with teaching, but He also performed amazing miracles. The first of His miracles was at a wedding where the groom ran into a huge problem. In those days, running out of wine was a huge embarrassment and shameful to the host—and this wedding was out of wine. So, Jesus stepped in. He literally turned water into wine—one drink turned into a completely different drink! No one had ever seen anything like this before. But, Jesus was just getting started on His mission, which would include many more astonishing miracles like this.

Jesus didn't perform miracles to get attention or simply to do something cool. These miracles He performed pointed to something greater—His identity as God's only Son, full of power and glory. Not many people knew He was the one who turned water into wine at the wedding, but His disciples knew, and they believed in Him. Seeing this miracle increased and strengthened their faith in the One they were following. Belief and faith are needed to follow Jesus and to begin a relationship with Him. When we surrender our life to Jesus, we do it by faith. We have faith that Jesus is who He says He is, and when we accept Him into our lives, a miracle takes place immediately. If you have accepted Jesus, you've already been a part of the greatest miracle you'll ever witness! Take a moment to celebrate and thank Jesus for the miracle of living in you.

delight |

How has seeing miracles or reading about them in the Bible increased your faith?

What differences have you noticed since accepting Jesus into your life? What is a noticeable way He has changed you?

display |

Accepting Jesus is a miracle. Take a moment to reflect about when you experienced the miracle of accepting Jesus in your heart, beginning your life as a follower of Jesus. Write down how this memory makes you feel.

Having Jesus in our hearts changes everything. It doesn't mean life automatically gets easy, but it does mean we receive a new identity, which is miraculous. Read 2 Corinthians 5:17: "Therefore, if anyone is in Christ, he is a new creation; the old has passed away, and see, the new has come!"

Spend a moment praising God for His miraculous power and faithfulness. Thank Him for the gift of the Bible, which provides truth, instructions, and stories of Jesus's miracles. Pray that you will have an increased desire to read the Word and that your faith will be built with Scripture you read. Thank Him for the ultimate miracle of having Jesus in your life. Pray to have an awareness of His presence throughout each day and to never take Him for granted. Pray for any family members you have that are not experiencing life with Jesus.

MIRACLES, MINISTRY, AND TEACHING

Three years. That's not even enough time to graduate high school! However, Jesus changed the world in three short years. He crammed a lifetime of miracles, ministry, and teaching into this short time frame. He changed lives. He flipped the script. He showed what true love looks like. Over the next two weeks, you will explore the highlights of these three years and see for yourself the awesome wonder of Jesus and the difference He has made and continues to make in the lives of billions.

DAY 9
ONE AND ONLY SON

discover |

READ JOHN 3:1-21.

For God loved the world in this way: He gave his one and only
Son, so that everyone who believes in him will not perish but
have eternal life. For God did not send his Son into the world
to condemn the world, but to save the world through him.
—John 3:16-17

God's love for the world is so great that He was willing to give up His one and only Son. He gave the world the best He had to offer. This was not a surprise to Him: God had planned it from the beginning. He knew that He would have to offer up His Son in order for us to have a restored relationship with Him and eternal life.

Jesus was sent into the world so that it could be saved through Him. Part of His mission while on earth was to tell others about Himself so that they could believe and experience a relationship with Him. Now, it's our turn. We are to tell others about who Jesus is and why He came to earth. What a great message we have the opportunity to share!

In the two short key verses, we see three important things: we are loved by God, saved by Jesus, and given eternal life. This is our reality as believers, but the same is not true for unbelievers. Jesus was clear on His mission to share with unbelievers so that they would become believers. His purpose for coming to earth was so that we could have a relationship with God and experience eternal life. His death, burial, and resurrection provide access to God for all who believe. God desires that all people will be saved. He doesn't desire to see anyone perish, and it's only through Jesus that we can be saved.

delight |

How would you feel if you didn't know about God's love for you and that Jesus came to save you?

What do you think your life would look like if you hadn't given your life to Jesus?

display |

God's love for you is so great. You can be assured of this by the gift that He gave you. Think about gifts you give to people. You give some people more valuable gifts than others. The amount you give usually reflects your relationship with them. God gave you His absolute best—His one and only Son. Jesus was clear on His mission: He came to save the world. There are many people in the world who don't know Him, and our mission is to tell others.

Who is Jesus and why did He come to earth?

Who will you share this good news with this week?

Take a few moments to focus on the meaning of the key verse. Spend time thanking God for anything that comes to mind, and ask for wisdom on how to bring Him glory in the way you live your life. Thank God for the love that He expressed when He sent Jesus into the world. Ask God to remind you throughout this week of His love for you and for the opportunity to share that love with others who need to hear about Jesus. Pray for people in your community who are unbelievers and need to hear the hope of the gospel.

DAY 10
WHOEVER

discover |

READ JOHN 4:1-26.

"But whoever drinks from the water that I will give him will
never get thirsty again. In fact, the water I will give him will
become a well of water springing up in him for eternal life."
—John 4:14

Have you seen people wear bracelets that say, "What would Jesus do?" That's a question we often ask as Christians, but let's take it a step further and take a look at what Jesus did, and then model it. In John 4, He went out of his way to meet the woman at the well.

Jesus didn't have much in common with her; they did not share the same gender, race, or religious views. At that time in their culture, those differences were a big deal! Just by speaking to her, Jesus could have been shunned by others. But He showed love for her despite their differences and the social risks He took.

Jesus was showing that those differences don't matter—He said "whoever drinks from the water that I will give him will never get thirsty again." He was showing that He isn't only available to certain people. Jesus came for all people, everywhere! He doesn't exclude people, and neither should we. In verse 14, Jesus made it clear that anyone who receives what He offers will have eternal life. Eternal life is a gift that we have from Jesus, and it is a gift that is available to all people in all places.

Jesus 101

delight |

Jesus went out of His way to meet the woman at the well. How can you go out of your way to meet someone that looks, speaks, and/or acts differently than you?

How does this story make you think about how you interact with those who look differently than you?

display |

Write down the names of three people that you don't know well and don't have much in common with. Take a moment to think about how you have treated them in the past. Do you typically ignore them, just say hi, gossip about them, or are you friendly to them?

Beside each name, write down one thing you can do today to model Jesus's behavior.

Spend a moment thanking God that He sent Jesus to save all people. Thank Him for the gift of eternal life that is available to anyone in the world who believes in Him. Ask Him to reveal any areas to you where you may treat people poorly based on your differences. Ask for forgiveness for your actions. Take a moment to thank God that He doesn't treat you poorly because you are different than Him. Ask Him to help you see others and treat others in a way that honors Him.

DAY 11

REJECTED

discover |

READ LUKE 4:16-30.

When they heard this, everyone in the synagogue was enraged. They
got up, drove him out of town, and brought him to the edge of the hill
that their town was built on, intending to hurl him over the cliff.
—Luke 4: 28-29

You will likely face rejection from others because of your belief in
Jesus. Many of us will be made fun of, be treated rudely, or be avoided
because we are Christians. There are times when our own friends or
family will have a hard time understanding why we live our lives the way
that we do. You may have experienced this—having people treat you
unfairly because you follow Jesus. We may have experienced rejection
in our lives, but it is nothing like what Jesus experienced in this passage.
They literally tried to throw Him off a cliff!

He read from Scripture and spoke truth about Himself, and people in
the synagogue were angry. They doubted Him because of where He was
from and because they knew His earthly father, Joseph. They looked
down on Him because they'd seen Him grow up and knew His family,
which led them to disqualify and reject Him. People who have known
you since you were a kid or even those related to you may not accept
that you pursue Jesus. They may not accept or understand that you take
your faith seriously. As you follow Jesus, you may experience rejection
from others, and that can hurt. Jesus faced this rejection early in His
ministry and continued to face it throughout His life on earth. If Jesus
faced rejection, you will, too. But He is with you, so be encouraged that
He accepts and loves you even when others reject you.

delight

How have you faced rejection because you are a Christ follower?

The world may reject you, but Jesus accepts you. How does that impact how you respond to rejection?

display |

Jesus faced rejection often, but didn't let it stop Him from His mission. If Jesus faced rejection, so will we. But we must remember our priority is to do the will of God and focus on Him.

Think about a time when you were rejected by others because of your belief in Jesus. How did you respond?

Read John 15:16, Romans 15:7, and 1 Peter 2:9

Knowing this is who God says you are, how does it help you respond to being rejected by others?

Spend a moment thinking about the omnipresence of God (meaning He is present everywhere). Thank Him that He will never leave you and is with you always, even when you face rejection. Share with God the pain you feel when you face rejection by others. Ask Him to replace the fears of rejection with boldness and faith that will allow you to walk in freedom.

Thank Jesus for His willingness to come to earth and be rejected over and over again so that you would be accepted by our holy God. Ask God to help you remember you are accepted and dearly loved by Him.

THE HEART OF THE MATTER

discover |

READ MATTHEW 5:21-30.

"You have heard that it was said, Do not commit adultery.
But I tell you, everyone who looks at a woman lustfully has
already committed adultery with her in his heart."
—Matthew 5:27-28

Some people call themselves rule-followers. It can be easy to get caught up in obeying the rules while neglecting why we follow the rules. Sometimes we obey the rules, but we do it with the wrong attitude. Are you like that, or do you know someone who is? Jesus is saying that simply obeying rules isn't enough; it's what's in our hearts that matters.

After reading these verses, many students will confidently say that they've never murdered anyone or committed adultery. However, it's not so easy to say they've never had hatred for someone or lust for someone. Jesus isn't simply worried about our actions, but the heart that guides our actions.

On the outside, we may look really "religious" to others by doing things like volunteering, going to church, or even taking your Bible to school— yet our hearts can still be far from Jesus. Many of us have been guilty of having actions that looked wholesome when our hearts weren't.

Jesus cares about what's in our hearts. Not only does He care, but He is serious about the sin we tolerate. We see this by how strongly He talks about hatred and lust. The state of your heart is important, and Jesus desires for you to honor Him even when there's no one watching.

delight |

Do you sometimes follow rules with the wrong motive?

Why is the condition of your heart so important?

display |

Sometimes we read the Bible and think Jesus is talking *at* us when it's beneficial to imagine being with Him and visualize Him talking *to* us. Imagine being in the crowd on the mountainside as Jesus was teaching. There's a huge crowd around Him, but He just made eye contact with you. He's speaking about the condition of your heart.

Take a moment to ask God to bring things to your mind that you have done "for" Him. Ask Him to reveal things that you have done for Him with the wrong motive. What is your response to what you've learned?

Thank God for His righteousness and His care for the condition of your heart. Confess anything that is keeping you from pursuing Him wholeheartedly. Pray for Godly friends who will provide accountability in this area. Ask for guidance and allow yourself to be vulnerable with God. Ask Him to reveal truth to you in this area by praying Psalm 139:23-24. "Search me, God, and know my heart; test me and know my concerns. See if there is any offensive way in me; lead me in the everlasting way." Pray for strength, wisdom, and a stronger desire to seek things that bring God glory.

DAY 13

THE NARROW GATE

discover |

READ MATTHEW 7:13-23.

"Enter through the narrow gate. For the gate is wide and the road broad
that leads to destruction, and there are many who go through it. How
narrow is the gate and difficult the road that leads to life, and few find it."
—Matthew 7:13-14

Narrow gate, difficult road, few find it—these are usually not the slogans people use to get others to join their cause. But the reality is, you probably have experienced challenging and difficult times as you have been on your journey following Jesus. If this has been your experience, you are truly following Him, and you're on the right path!

Jesus understands that following Him isn't always easy. You probably see people at school "follow the crowd" down a different road. The reality is, that road may look fun, but it leads to destruction. God's plan for you is not destruction, but to bear good fruit.

You will face challenges as you follow Jesus, but following Him is worth it, and it produces fruit in your life. Fruit isn't produced by simply going to church, owning a Bible, or because your family members are strong Christians. Sometimes we think those things show that we are Christians, but it's the fruit in our lives that speaks for us.

We can all agree that it's not always easy going through the narrow gate, but Jesus didn't guarantee us an easy life. He did, however, guarantee that we have eternal life through Him. His desire for you is to enter through the narrow gate and experience not an easy life, but eternal life.

delight |

What fruit do you see being produced in your life?

How does the fruit in your life point to your decision to enter through the narrow gate?

display

Fruit is produced as we grow and mature spiritually. It changes our lives and allows us to impact and help others. Read Galatians 5:22-23.

> *22 But the fruit of the Spirit is love, joy, peace, patience, kindness, goodness, faithfulness, 23 gentleness, and self-control. The law is not against such things.*

Think about a time you've experienced the fruit of someone else. Has someone been patient with you when you were struggling, shown you kindness on a bad day, or shown you gentleness when you were hurting? How did that bless you?

How will you be more intentional this week, allowing your fruit to help those around you?

Thank God for allowing you to be used to produce fruit for His glory. Spend a moment thanking Him for the times you've been impacted from other believers bearing fruit.

Ask for the fruit in your life to be evident to everyone you meet. Pray for God to help you as you desire for your life to reflect love, joy, peace, patience, kindness, goodness, faithfulness, gentleness, and self-control. Ask God to bring people into your path that need a Godly example and to bring other Christians in your life to encourage you and help you as you go through the narrow gate.

IN THE STORM

discover |

READ LUKE 8:22-25.

They came and woke him up, saying, "Master, Master, we're going to die!"
—Luke 8:24a

No matter how much you like storms, they can be frightening at times. It seems like the storm that came while the disciples were in the boat was of the pretty big, scary variety. They were panicking, and Jesus was asleep. They woke Him up because they were afraid they would lose their lives in the storm, but Jesus had already told them they would go to the other side of the lake (v. 22). So basically, Jesus already let them know that they would arrive safely.

While you probably can't relate to being on a boat in the middle of a storm, you probably have experienced other storms in your life. We experience storms in many different ways—it could be our health, seeing a loved one struggle with sickness, friendship issues, or problems at home or school. Like the disciples, sometimes we find it hard to trust God when we are in the middle of a storm. Although the disciples were scared in the storm, they still did the right thing—they knew who to go to. They knew if anyone could do something about the storm, it was Jesus. When you experience a storm in life, do what the disciples did and go to Jesus. He has never failed, and you can trust that He will never leave you alone. He is with you during every storm of life.

delight |

List three people you trust. Beside each name, write out why you trust them.

1.

2.

3.

How can you grow in your trust of Jesus?

display |

Take a moment and think about the worst storm you've been through in your life. How did you handle it? We never know what storms lie ahead for us. The disciples' faith was tested during the storm. The next time your faith is tested, recall this story and be reminded that Jesus is with you in the middle of the storm. Remember that Jesus may not always calm the storm, but He will be with you through it.

How can you be encouraged when you face your next storm?

Write down three reasons Jesus is trustworthy.

1.

2.

3.

Thank Jesus that He is with you right now. He's with you in times of sunshine and in the middle of a storm. Ask Him to help you trust Him even more and that you would feel His peace surrounding you. Ask Him to grow your faith and increase your trust so that not only your life will be impacted, but that you will impact others in your family and community. Be reminded that He has never failed and He never will; nothing is too hard for Him, nothing is greater, nothing has more power, and no one loves you more than Him.

JESUS

said to her,

"I am the resurrection and the life. The one who believes in me, even if he dies, will live."

DAY 15

A LOT WITH A LITTLE

discover |

READ MARK 6:30-44.

He took the five loaves and the two fish, and looking up to heaven, he blessed and broke the loaves. He kept giving them to his disciples to set before the people. He also divided the two fish among them all. Everyone ate and was satisfied.
—Mark 6:41-42

The Bible is full of miracles, and it's fun to read and hear about them. Let's be honest: it can be a lot easier to believe the miracles we read in the Bible and not believe that God can work miracles in our lives. Have you felt that way before? As believers, we are actually called to believe, right? However, our belief is limited when we aren't willing to be used by Jesus. We must believe that Jesus works miracles in us and through us. Jesus hasn't stopped performing miracles and can perform miraculous works through you when you're submitted to Him.

The crowd was over five thousand men—not including women and children—and Jesus took something so small to feed so many. This story may be familiar to you, but please take a moment to think about how amazing it is. Thousands of people were hungry, fed, and satisfied with five loaves, two fish, and Jesus's desire to meet their needs. He wants to meet your needs as well. Give Him all you have to offer, even if it feels small. We tend to hold back because we think we don't have enough to offer, but Jesus desires for us to follow Him wholeheartedly and be willing to be used in His miraculous story.

In this story, Jesus did a lot with a little. Give Him the little you have and watch Him do a lot with it.

delight

How would you have reacted to being in the crowd and being fed by Jesus? Would it have changed your belief in Jesus?

What recent miracle have you read about or seen lately? How does that build your faith?

display

We sometimes believe miraculous things when they happen to others, but disqualify ourselves from witnessing or being a part of a miracle.

Are you weak or strong when it comes to believing miracles can happen in your life?

If you feel weak, think of two reasons why you feel this way. Text your small group leader or youth pastor and ask if you can meet with them to begin studying the miracles of Jesus.

Praise God for His wonderful, mighty, and miraculous works. Praise Him for how Jesus took something so small, fed thousands, and still had leftovers. Pray that any barriers that are holding you back from giving your all will be removed. Pray for boldness to give your all and for God to increase your faith so that you will have the opportunity to share with others about the miraculous works of Jesus. Ask God for a fresh excitement about being used for His glory. Pray for the opportunity to see or be a part of a miracle this week.

DAY 16

HOW TO WALK ON WATER

discover |

READ MATTHEW 14:22-33.

When they got into the boat, the wind ceased. Then those in the boat worshiped him and said, "Truly you are the Son of God."
—Matthew 14:32-33

Are there times in your life when you've handled situations like Peter? Maybe you had courage to take the first step and then looked around at the circumstances and allowed yourself to be filled with fear. Have you ever experienced that?

While Jesus hasn't called us to literally walk on water like Peter, He has invited us to walk in faith as Peter did. We see that Peter accomplished the impossible when his eyes were focused on Jesus. When he took his eyes off of Jesus and began to focus on the situation around him, he began to sink.

Jesus shows us that even when we doubt and begin to sink, He is right there to rescue us. It is only because He is the one true Son of God that He even has the power to rescue you. You can always call out to Jesus when you are sinking because He is present, powerful, and your Savior.

The disciples began to realize this as well. They may not have previously understood everything about Him, but after this miracle, they worshiped Him as the Son of God. They had been following Jesus closely and witnessed many miracles, but on this stormy night in the middle of the sea, they saw faith in action. They witnessed ordinary Peter walk on the water to Jesus and responded in the only way they knew how: worship.

delight

If you were in the boat, would you have asked to step out of the boat? Why or why not?

Jesus immediately reached out to Peter. When was the last time you felt Jesus reaching out to you?

display

The disciples acknowledged Jesus as the Son of God after this miracle. On day 14 of this devotional, you read about Jesus calming the storm. After that miracle, the disciples asked, "Who then is this? He commands even the winds and the waves, and they obey him!" (Luke 8:25). This time at sea, they now understood who He was and responded by worshiping Him.

In what ways will you worship Jesus today?

What are two areas in your life where fear is keeping you "in the boat?"

Read 1 Peter 5:7 and Psalm 34:4. Write down how these verses change your perspective on what you fear.

Thank Jesus that He not only calms the storm, but calls you to walk in faith during the storm. Ask Him to increase your faith where it is weak and show you areas where you need to "get out of the boat." Ask Him to help you respond in obedience and point others to Him. Thank Jesus for the love that He has for you and His willingness to rescue you when you are sinking. Ask Him to forgive you for the times you let fear keep you from being obedient.

DAY 17
BREAD OF LIFE

discover |

READ JOHN 6:22-69.

Then they said, "Sir, give us this bread always." "I am the bread of life," Jesus told them. "No one who comes to me will ever be hungry, and no one who believes in me will ever be thirsty again."
—John 6:34–35

The crowd was looking for Jesus because they wanted something from Him, but what they wanted was temporary and would not satisfy. He explained that if they were willing to believe in Him, they would be filled for eternity. Jesus's teaching was not well received by the crowd. They were looking for a quick, temporary fix, but He offered so much more. While Jesus wasn't opposed to meeting their physical needs, His priority was meeting their spiritual need, which was belief in Him.

The crowd wanted a resource, but Jesus is the source. Sometimes we are guilty of the same thing—we tend to forget that Jesus is the source and that we must depend on Him completely. In our country, with plenty of resources, we can find it challenging to rely on Him, but He is everything we need. In Him, we have abundant life on earth and eternal life after we experience death on earth.

We should spiritually depend on Jesus daily, just like we physically depend on food daily. When we offer ourselves to Him and "eat" from the portion He gives us, we will sustained because He is the Bread of Life.

delight

Do you find it challenging to depend completely on Jesus as your source? How do you acknowledge Him as your source and not just the one who fixes your temporary need?

In what ways are you tempted to rely on yourself instead of Jesus to have your needs met?

display

We are busy people, and it can be easy to go throughout the day and not consider your need for Jesus. Today, remember that He is your source and that you need Him more than anything—even food.

Google today's key verse and make it your phone's lock screen or background to remind you that Jesus is the Bread of Life, or write the verse on an index card and keep it close by.

Let each meal you eat today serve as a reminder to depend on Him. At each meal you eat today, grab your phone or index card with the verses on it and read them. Say a prayer asking Him to help you depend on Him more.

Thank Jesus for being the Bread of Life and inviting you to depend on Him. Praise Him for being dependable, trustworthy, loving, and kind. Confess any times that you have lived on your terms, forgetting that He is the source of everything. Share with Him any doubts you have or areas you're struggling to trust Him in. Ask Him to remind you to lean on and trust Him in all things. Pray for those in your community who are trusting in their resources and not the Source. Ask God for opportunities for you to share Jesus with them.

DAY 18

LISTEN TO HIM

discover |

READ MATTHEW 17:1-13.

While he was still speaking, suddenly a bright cloud covered
them, and a voice from the cloud said, "This is my beloved
Son, with whom I am well-pleased. Listen to him!"
—Matthew 17:5

Jesus took Peter, James, and John up a mountain where they witnessed a miracle. Jesus was joined by Elijah and Moses while Peter, James, and John witnessed and were also able to hear the voice of God. They saw a glimpse of the eternal glory that is in store for those who belong to God's kingdom. They actually heard God speaking, acknowledging Jesus as His Son, which would remove any doubt about who they were following. His disciples were assured that they were indeed in the presence of Jesus, the only Son of God.

They were impacted by this experience, but Jesus was affected as well. He was soon to be headed to the cross, and experiencing this moment served as a powerful reminder of the life and glory in heaven He would soon return to. He was able to be edified in front of His disciples by His Father who expressed His love and pleasure with Him.

He knew that anguish, pain, betrayal, and death on a cross was coming soon, but He followed through with the plan put in place by His Father. Hearing His Father grant authority and express His love and pleasure with Him gave Him confidence to complete the plan to restore our broken relationship with God.

delight |

Although we see that Jesus was loved by God, God's only Son, that He pleased God, and has authority, do you find it hard to listen to and follow Him? Why or why not?

God's plan for Jesus was to mend your broken relationship with God. How can you participate in this plan to help mend the broken relationship of others with God?

display |

This story is full of miracles, and we see how powerful and perfect God is. Write down one miracle from the story that stood out the most to you.

God publicly acknowledged Jesus as His Son; God said He was pleased and that we should listen to Jesus. How are you listening to and following Jesus? What is one thing you know Jesus wants you to do? Write one way you can accomplish this task this week.

Praise God for His power, glory, love, and presence.

Take a moment to think about Jesus's willingness to leave His home in heaven, come to earth, and die a brutal death to fulfill God's plan. Ask God to help you live in full awareness of Jesus's sacrifice and to help you follow Him more closely. Ask for forgiveness if there have been times when you took His sacrifice for granted.

Pray for those who don't know the love, glory, and plan of the Father and for opportunities to share Jesus with them.

DAY 19
NOT TOO FAR

READ LUKE 15:11-32.

So he got up and went to his father. But while the son was still a
long way off, his father saw him and was filled with compassion.
He ran, threw his arms around his neck, and kissed him.
—Luke 15:20

There can be times in our lives when we wander away from what we know to be true. We can drift from God if we don't put Him first, and poor decisions will likely follow. Does that sound familiar to you? Have you ever felt far from God because of guilt and shame about things you've done?

We see in this story that the son made poor choices, but he ended up making the right choice by going back to his father, admitting he was wrong, and receiving forgiveness.

This story shows us how God responds when we return to Him after turning away. When you admit your sin and return to God, just know that He is not sitting in heaven waiting for you to return so that He can yell at you. God is like the father in this story, and He wants to celebrate that you are returning to Him. In fact, the father in this story was looking for his son because he noticed him when he was still a long way off.

No matter what you've done or where you've been, you are not too far from God. He can't love you any more or any less than He does right now. He is your perfect Father who loves you unconditionally and extends grace and mercy to you.

delight

Have you allowed guilt to keep you from feeling comfortable praying to or worshiping God? How can you overcome this feeling if or when you have it?

How does this story encourage you? What does it make you feel toward God?

display |

Take a moment to think about something you've done that you know did not please God. Have you allowed it to create distance between you and God? If so, write it down.

Admit to Him that you sinned and ask for forgiveness.

Receive His forgiveness and imagine yourself in the story and God running towards you, throwing His arms around you, and kissing you.

Spend time thanking God that He loves and forgives you even when you drift away. Take a moment to thank Him that He is always available, with arms wide open, a big smile, with all the love in His heart, ready to celebrate when you return, and welcome you home no matter what. Ask God to help you forgive yourself if that's an area you're struggling in. Be reminded that this is an awesome story that points to the awesome response of a father welcoming his son home. Spend quiet time with God thinking about how you are a picture of the son and God is a picture of the father.

DAY 20

GRACE, HOPE, AND FORGIVENESS

discover |

READ JOHN 8:2-11.

When Jesus stood up, he said to her, "Woman, where are they? Has no one condemned you?" "No one, Lord," she answered. "Neither do I condemn you," said Jesus. "Go, and from now on do not sin anymore."
—John 8:10-11

It's so easy to point out the sin in other people's lives. Two things are true: we all sin, and we all need forgiveness. May we as Christians never be the first to pick up a stone attempting to punish someone for their sin as the people in this story did.

There is so much we see in this story: sin, humiliation, grace, hope, and forgiveness. We see a woman in desperate need of grace while others are ready to stone her. We often find it easier to pick up a stone and publicly point out other people's sin, but as Christians, we are to point them to Jesus instead, because He offers forgiveness. Isn't that what we all need? You know that feeling you get when you've done something wrong and you've been caught? What do you desire most in that moment? Forgiveness.

Jesus offers grace, not condemnation. We can all relate to the woman in the story. She was a sinner who deserved death before she met Jesus, and so were we. Jesus came to earth so that we could be forgiven; however, we must take His forgiveness and grace seriously and "Go and sin no more." Does this mean you will never sin again? Not at all. It just means the desire of our hearts and lives should be to leave sin behind us and live for the One who saved us.

Jesus 101

delight |

Who are you in the story? The person with stone or the person needing forgiveness? Explain.

What is something you need to repent of?

display |

Jesus came to forgive sinners, and He models that in this story. As sinful human beings, our natural instinct is not forgiveness. Instead, we sometimes find ourselves wanting to "throw stones." We are called to model Jesus's behavior and offer grace, hope, and forgiveness.

Who do you need to apologize to for "throwing stones" at them? Ask God for forgiveness, then seek to create an opportunity to sit down with them and ask for forgiveness in person.

Who do you need to forgive? Take a moment to pray about the situation. Ask God to help you move past bitterness and hurt and live in the freedom of forgiveness.

Thank God for the truth found in 1 John 1:9: "If we confess our sins, He is faithful and righteous to forgive us our sins and to cleanse us from all unrighteousness." Thank Him for being faithful, righteous, and forgiving. Ask Him to help you see others as forgiven and loved and to resist the urge to "throw stones," but to have compassion instead. Pray for those who have been hurt by believers who "threw stones" at them and did not comfort or show them the love of Jesus. Ask the Lord to help you maintain a tender heart for others.

DAY 21

BACK TO LIFE

discover |

READ JOHN 11:1-44.

Jesus said to her, "I am the resurrection and the life. The
one who believes in me, even if he dies, will live."
—John 11:25

Can you imagine what it was like to be in the crowd that day? To see someone you know be brought back to life and walk out of the grave? This miracle was to prove to the crowd that Jesus had the power to raise the dead. Ultimately, He tells us that those who believe in Him would be raised from the dead as well, meaning they will experience eternal life. To have eternal life means to live in heaven with Jesus even after you die on earth. Some people in the crowd believed and some did not, but He wanted them to see that He had power even over death. People who witnessed this miracle would likely find it easier to believe in His own resurrection, which was coming soon.

Jesus stood at Lazarus's tomb knowing that He would soon be in a tomb Himself. But there was a major difference between what happened to Lazarus and what would happen to Jesus. Tragically, one day Lazarus would have to die... again. For Jesus, after His resurrection, He would never die again. He would be the first born from the dead (Col. 1:18).

Jesus proved that He has the power to bring someone back to life, but He also said that He IS the resurrection. There is life in Jesus, and if you are His follower, you will experience eternal life after you leave this earth in addition to abundant life while you're still on earth.

delight |

What does Lazarus's resurrection say about Jesus?

Why is eternal life important?

display |

Read Revelation 21:4; 22:1-2, 5.

Write down three things that stand out to you from those verses. Next to each thing listed, write down why it stood out to you. Put this list in on a mirror you look at daily so that it will be a daily reminder of the gift you have to look forward to because of your belief in Jesus.

Spend a moment praising Jesus for His power that is stronger than anything in this world, even death. Thank God for the amazing gift of eternal life that you will experience as a believer. Pray by name for two people who don't understand the gift of eternal life. Pray that their hearts will be softened and that a door would be opened for them to hear and receive the gospel. Ask God to reveal Himself to you this week as you ponder the list describing what eternal life will be like for you.

DAY 22

SEEK AND SAVE

discover |

READ LUKE 19:1-10.

"Today salvation has come to this house," Jesus told him, "because he too is a son of Abraham. For the Son of Man has come to seek and to save the lost."
—Luke 19:9-10

Zacchaeus was known by others as a sinful man, so why would Jesus choose to have dinner at his home? Because it was His mission—it's the very thing He came to do. Jesus came for people like Zacchaeus, people you know at school, and for you. None of us were born Christians. We were all born separated from God. We were lost, and Jesus said the lost are who He came for.

Have you ever wondered what it means to say that Jesus came to seek and save the lost? *Seek* means to look for. *Save* means to rescue. The lost are people headed for eternal destruction.

Jesus's purpose on earth was to look for and rescue people headed for eternal destruction. Zacchaeus was headed for destruction, but his life changed when he met Jesus.

After being noticed in the tree, Jesus began a conversation with Zacchaeus and spent time with him. This shows us that Jesus sees and notices us no matter where we are, and He wants to spend time with us.

He completed His mission on earth, and now we have the opportunity to pick up where He left off. We have the opportunity to notice others, spend time with them, and introduce them to Jesus.

delight

How did salvation come to Zacchaeus?

Zacchaeus showed repentance. What wrongs in your life do you need to repent of and seek to make right?

display

Jesus was making His way through the town of Jericho when He noticed Zacchaeus. He didn't simply notice him and keep going, but He stopped, had a conversation, and spent time with him. Being noticed by Jesus changed Zacchaeus's life. It didn't only change his life on earth, but it changed his eternity. He was now able to identify as a follower of Jesus, and it started by being noticed. In our culture today, we are so busy that we rarely stop to notice or spend time with people.

How will you slow down today to notice, converse with, and spend time with someone today?

Praise Jesus for who He is and for noticing you even as you read this devotional right now. Ponder His greatness. Thank Him for being present in your life and noticing every detail about you. Thank Him for His willingness to fulfill His mission to seek and save the lost. Take a moment to remember what it was like when you were lost. Pray for the lost people at your school. Ask God to give you sensitivity to notice them and the opportunity to spend time with them so that you can be used to bring them into His family of believers.

SECTION 3

THE END IS ONLY THE BEGINNING

For most tales, when you come to the words "The End," that means the story is over. This is not the case with Jesus. The last week of His earthly life was eventful, painful, and tragic, but ultimately triumphant. The final eight days of this book will explore this short time, but when it's over, it'll only have just begun.

FROM PRAISE TO REJECTION

discover |

READ MARK 11:1-10.

Blessed is the coming kingdom of our father David!
Hosanna in the highest heaven!
—Mark 11:10

This passage details the beginning of Jesus's last week on earth prior to His crucifixion. Jesus was welcomed into Jerusalem by a crowd of people who were worshiping, celebrating, and honoring Him. There stood a loud mass of people giving Him the greeting of a king as they laid out a "red carpet" for Him, laying their coats and branches in the streets. They shouted praises and called Him blessed, knowing He was worthy. It was a beautiful way to honor Jesus, but days later the same crowd rejected Him. The crowd found it easy to praise Him when they thought He would rule the way they desired, but when Jesus didn't fulfill their idea of a king, they rejected Him.

The faces of people who were celebrating Him were the same faces that demanded He be crucified only a few days later. It's so easy to read this Scripture and wonder why they acted this way, but if we're honest, we have likely praised Jesus in church before and then refused to admit we're a Christian at school in front of others.

If we aren't careful, our actions can be closely aligned to the people in this story. We must be careful that our praises to Jesus aren't based simply on what He will do for us or reserved for only one day of the week. Jesus deserves the best of our praise every day.

delight |

Why do we praise Jesus unashamedly at church but get quiet about Him when we're in front of a different crowd?

Outside of time at church, how does your life reflect genuine worship to Jesus?

display

What will you do daily to ensure you aren't reserving your praises to Jesus for only one day a week? If you need options, pick two things from the list you can incorporate into your life this week.

- ☐ **Listen to worship music**

- ☐ **Pray**

- ☐ **Read the Bible for ten minutes**

- ☐ **Read a devotional (like this one)**

- ☐ **Spend five minutes in silence with God**

- ☐ **Work on memorizing Scripture**

- ☐ **Write down three things you are thankful for daily.**

Fill in the blanks below with the two things you will do.

> **Because praising Jesus is important to me, I plan to spend time with Him daily by _____ and _____.**

Praise Jesus for His kindness, patience, and grace that He extends to you. Ask Him to help you seek Him daily. Take time to talk to Jesus about reasons you may struggle with not being consistent with your praises. Share any obstacles, distractions, or peer pressure that may keep you from pursuing Him every day of the week. Ask Him to increase your desire to seek Him. Pray for an increased desire to read and follow His Word, to spend more time filling your mind with worship music and prayer. Thank Him for the opportunity to invite Him into your day.

LEAD BY SERVING

discover

READ JOHN 13:1-17.

*"So if I, your Lord and Teacher, have washed your feet, you
also ought to wash one another's feet. For I have given you an
example, that you also should do just as I have done for you."*
—John 13:14–15

There are tons of books on the topic of leadership, but the Bible is the best one of all. We can learn many lessons of leadership from Jesus as He led by example. During His time on earth, He loved, led, and served.

In this story, Jesus did something no one else in the room cared to do—He served His disciples by washing their feet. This was the lowliest of jobs. Jesus, the King of kings, the Highest of the high, knelt down to a low position and served His friends. Jesus gives us a great example of what it means to lead by serving.

Most people like to be served, but few people like *to* serve. Serving doesn't usually come naturally for us. Not many of us jump at the chance to wash dishes at home or pick up trash after a football game. The cool thing about serving is that we are modeling Jesus when we serve— especially when we clean up a mess we didn't make. He came to this earth to clean up a mess He didn't make.

Whether it's picking up trash at a lunch table, doing chores around the house without being asked, or literally washing someone's feet, it's all about our motive—and our motive is to model Jesus. Spending time serving will be time spent that you will not regret.

delight |

What is your favorite way to serve others?

How do you feel after serving someone in need?

display

Jesus teaches us a lesson on how to lead by serving others. You have the opportunity to point to Jesus even when you're hanging out with friends. Take the lead in your friend group and be known as the one who serves others. You have the opportunity to influence your peers. By watching you, their hearts may be stirred to serve as well!

What are two ways you plan to serve this week at home?

What are two ways you plan to serve this week at school?

Praise Jesus for the selfless life of serving He led. Thank Him for the opportunity you have to point to Him by serving those around you. Give thanks for the example He left by showing us the importance of serving. Ask for the desire to serve your family, friends, and community. Ask for forgiveness for any times you ignored the call to serve others. Pray for help to overcome any obstacles that are keeping you from serving and to show you opportunities to serve others.

DAY 25

THE HARD THINGS

discover |

READ LUKE 22:39-46.

"Father, if you are willing, take this cup away from me — nevertheless, not my will, but yours, be done."
—Luke 22:42

Jesus had only hours to live. He knew pain was ahead, and it grieved Him. It grieved Him so much that He asked God if there was another way. There was not, and He courageously surrendered to God's plan, which ultimately brought God glory.

Although He was about to encounter agony and the weight of every sin ever committed, He faced crucifixion with courage. It took courage to go to the cross—an innocent man being tortured for the guilty. Ultimately, it was for God's glory. There was only one way for guilty people to be redeemed—a sacrifice equal to the cost. Jesus became this sacrifice for the cost of our sin. He took on our punishment.

God is glorified when we do the hard or uncomfortable things He leads us to do. Jesus had a hard assignment, and He responded with courage and completed it. You can be encouraged that with Jesus living inside you, you will have the courage you need to take your next step of obedience, even when you're facing the hardest situations. God asks us to endure hard things so that He will be glorified. He doesn't ask you to suffer just to suffer. There's always a bigger purpose, and even if you can't see it immediately, it will give God glory.

delight |

Jesus asked for the "cup to pass," but still endured it for our sake. How does that impact your decision-making?

What does Jesus's willingness to take on the cross reveal about how He feels about you?

display |

Read the key verse slowly. Jesus prayed from a place of agony, asking the Father to let the cup pass; however, He courageously accepted the wrath He didn't deserve. Because Jesus showed such courage, you can face hard things with courage, too, because His Spirit lives inside you.

Think back to a situation where you lacked courage. How does today's reading encourage you for the next time you face a battle?

Write John 16:33 in the space provided. Come back to this verse for the next seven days. Read it, dwell on it, and let it encourage you.

Give Jesus thanks for His courageous sacrifice and surrendering His will, following God's. Share with Jesus the areas in your life where you lack courage. Ask Him to build your courage as you confidently point others to Him. Ask Him to help you be strong and courageous and not to fear because He goes with you. Thank God that He will never leave you nor forsake you.

Thank Jesus for being willing to take the cup you deserved. Praise God for being with you as you go through the hard things because they are all for His glory.

DAY 26

ALONE

discover |

READ MATTHEW 26:47-56.

His betrayer had given them a sign: "The one I kiss, he's the one; arrest him." So immediately he went up to Jesus and said, "Greetings, Rabbi!" and kissed him.
—*Matthew 26:48-49*

Judas gave the sign of a kiss, which sealed his betrayal. He was a disciple who had traveled with Jesus, witnessed miracles, ate with Him, and "followed" Him….and he somehow found it easy to betray Jesus.

Not only had Jesus been betrayed by one of His disciples, but He was left alone by the other eleven disciples who should have stood by His side. They disappeared when Jesus was in the process of being arrested, leaving Him alone to face a mob of people with weapons. Think about the intensity of that night. Jesus had been betrayed and left alone in His most difficult hour. There were no longer thirteen men on one team; only one man was left standing…by Himself.

Jesus's disciples were His absolute closest friends, and they fled. If Jesus faced having friends who were not loyal at all times, it's likely you will face the same thing. Even if your closest friends leave you when you face hard situations, as a follower of Jesus, you can rest knowing you won't face them alone. Jesus is always within you, and you are never alone. He endured being alone in this moment and being alone on the cross so that you never have to endure separation from Him. He is faithful and loyal. He loves you and is with you always.

delight |

How have you dealt with being betrayed or left alone by a friend?

How do you think Jesus felt that night when it happened to Him?

display

Jesus's closest friends left Him as He was in the process of being arrested. Sometimes our friends don't make the best choices either, but Jesus is a friend to us like no other. He will never leave you, even if you're the friend who didn't make the right choice.

What obstacles may be in the way of you believing this is true?

Think back to a time when you felt betrayed or alone. Read Matthew 28:19-20. Although you felt alone, based on verse 20, where was Jesus the whole time?

Write the last sentence of Matthew 28:20 on a piece of paper or use a tablet or computer to graphically design it. Then print it out and put it on your bathroom mirror to serve as a reminder that Jesus is always with you.

> Praise God for His glory, dominion, and power. Thank Him for being present with you even when you didn't feel it. Share with God if you've had friends leave or betray you. Be honest with God about how that impacted your faith and your outlook on life. Ask Him to remind you the next time you're "alone" that you are not alone because He's with you. Share that you want to experience more of His presence and to grow in your friendship with Him. Praise Him for being the friend who sticks closer than a brother (Prov. 18:24) and will never leave or forsake you.

So if I, your Lord and Teacher, have washed your feet, you also ought to wash one another's feet.

JOHN 13:14-15

For I have given you an example,
that you also should do just
as I have done for you.

DAY 27

ALWAYS AVAILABLE

READ MATTHEW 26:69-75.

> *Then he started to curse and to swear with an oath, "I don't know*
> *the man!" Immediately a rooster crowed, and Peter remembered*
> *the words Jesus had spoken, "Before the rooster crows, you will*
> *deny me three times." And he went outside and wept bitterly.*
> *—Matthew 26:74-75*

Earlier in this very same chapter, Peter was adamant that he would never deny Jesus, saying that even if everyone else did, he would be willing to die before doing so. But things changed quickly. Soldiers arrived with weapons, ready to arrest Jesus, and Peter quickly changed his mind. Peter did, in fact, deny Jesus. Three times.

Peter was so bold about his faith one minute, and then hours later, failed. Even though it's hard to admit, we have likely been like Peter at times—declaring our faithfulness to Jesus one moment and then letting that moment pass when things got hard.

The blessing of failing in this way is that God forgives you when you repent. Peter truly was sorry for his denial. He was so sorry that he no longer had words, only tears. The best feeling of all is receiving God's forgiveness for our sins. God is concerned about the posture of our hearts. In order to receive forgiveness, we have to admit we were wrong and believe in Jesus's power and love that covers our sin. No matter what sin you've committed, forgiveness is always available for you. Because of Jesus's love for you, His forgiveness will allow you to walk in freedom and no longer be held by guilt or shame from your sin. Forgiveness is available—you just have to ask.

delight |

In what ways can you relate to Peter?

What would it be like to live in a world with no forgiveness? How does that inspire you to be a person who forgives?

display

After Jesus's arrest, Peter followed Him from a distance, denied knowing Him three times, and then the rooster crowed. Peter was reminded of Jesus's words, predicting his denial. What an intense moment! Peter wept bitterly.

Are you remorseful about the sin in your life?

Write a prayer of confession to God of any unconfessed sin.

Praise God for the grace and love He pours out on His children. Praise Him for the gift of forgiveness that was purchased by sending His Son to the cross. Thank Him for His loyalty despite the times you have denied Him in front of others or have denied the invitation to be led by Him in your decisions. Thank God for His love, patience, and the forgiveness that is available upon repentance. Pray for your heart to be sensitive to sin and that you would repent quickly and turn from sinful behavior. Pray for others who are struggling to ask for and receive the forgiveness available from God to them.

DAY 28
IT IS FINISHED

discover |

READ JOHN 19:16-30.

When Jesus had received the sour wine, he said, "It is finished." Then bowing his head, he gave up his spirit.
—John 19:30

Jesus was an innocent man who lived a sinless life in order to pay the penalty for guilty and sinful people. The story of Jesus dying on the cross should always excite you because it is the one event that changed the entire world.

We deserved death because of our sin, but Jesus took our punishment. Through His sacrifice on the cross, He accomplished everything we need for salvation. Salvation means to be saved or delivered from something; Jesus saved us from the eternal punishment for our sins.

His one sacrifice was sufficient. There's nothing we can do to add to our salvation. We can't be "good enough" or try to earn our way to heaven. He completed what we couldn't; only Jesus's sacrifice is the answer to our broken relationship with God. His sacrifice is enough.

He came to earth to complete His assignment. Knowing without any doubt He had fulfilled His job, He said, "It is finished," and gave up His Spirit. His words, "It is finished," tell us that the work was completed, permanent, and sufficient. What work did He complete? He completely paid the price for people from all nations to receive something they could never achieve on their own—salvation. If you have accepted Jesus, you can rest knowing He completely paid the price for your sin.

delight |

Why are you unable to achieve salvation apart from Jesus?

Since salvation is a gift that can't be earned, why do we find ourselves trying to working for it?

display

Jesus didn't save Himself from the cross because He chose to save you. He completed the work, and there is nothing you could do in your power to save yourself.

What are some ways you find yourself tempted to try and "earn" your salvation?

Does the temptation to try to do so increase when you know you've sinned and you need forgiveness?

In what ways can you be reminded that there's no need to "earn" it because Jesus says, "It is finished?"

Praise God for His redemption plan that makes salvation possible. Praise Him for His kindness and love. Thank God that you have been saved by grace and for the gift of salvation. Ponder the fact that it can't be earned and take a moment to confess if you've been guilty of trying to earn the gift that has been freely given. Ask Jesus to forgive you for trying to add to the work He already completed on the cross. Pray for family members or people you know who don't know the love of Jesus.

GONE AHEAD

discover |

READ MATTHEW 28:1-10.

"He is not here. For he has risen, just as he said. Come and see the place where he lay. Then go quickly and tell his disciples, 'He has risen from the dead and indeed he is going ahead of you to Galilee; you will see him there.' Listen, I have told you."
—Matthew 28:6-7

Can you imagine this scene? The disciples and all of Jesus's followers were grieving, lost, confused, and some were fearful because of His death. After three days of silence, that Sunday morning, they finally came to realize what Jesus had been talking about all along. He had told them of His death and resurrection many times, and they were finally able to see firsthand what He meant. This exciting day not only changed those who were friends with Jesus, but it changed the world forever!

The resurrection of Jesus is where He sealed the deal and where we are made righteous. He rose from the grave, conquering death and showing He has ultimate power and authority. Because of Jesus's position as the King of kings, we don't have to be afraid of anything—not even death.

The angel said Jesus had already gone ahead to Galilee, where He planned to meet the disciples. Jesus had already gone ahead of them. You can be assured and you don't have to be afraid of what's to come because Jesus has already gone ahead of you as well. You may be fearing an upcoming test, a medical diagnosis, or simply fearing starting something new. Be reminded that you don't have to fear what's to come because Jesus is with you, and He has already gone ahead of you.

delight |

What did Jesus prove by rising from the dead?

What comfort does it bring you knowing that Jesus has already gone ahead of you?

display

Jesus told the disciples many times that He would be buried and raised to life again. However, when the disciples saw Jesus crucified, they were shocked, distraught, and disappointed.

Recall a situation when you could relate to how the disciples felt.

Jesus has gone ahead of you, so you have no need to fear. List three things you are fearful of and then pray over each one, asking God to remove your fears and be reminded that Jesus is with you.

Praise Jesus as you are reminded of His power over death, His ability to be with you and ahead of you at the same time, and His great love for you, dying in your place. Confess any fears you may be struggling with. Share with Him why you are afraid and ask to be filled with His courage and boldness and to increase your faith and belief in Him. Thank Him for providing comfort for your fears and joy when you have tears. Pray for those who may be struggling with any fears or anxiety today.

DAY 30
WITH YOU

discover |

READ MATTHEW 28:19-20.

"Go, therefore, and make disciples of all nations, baptizing them in the name of the Father and of the Son and of the Holy Spirit, teaching them to observe everything I have commanded you. And remember, I am with you always, to the end of the age."
—Matthew 28:19-20

Before departing earth, Jesus made a promise: He would be with us until the end of the age, which means forever and always. Jesus will never leave you, not even for the tiniest moment. You can rest knowing His presence is with you as you complete the work He's called you to do.

He's called you to carry on the work that He started. His return to heaven didn't mean the work stopped, it meant He passed it along to us. We have the calling and privilege to share the message of Jesus, making disciples, baptizing, and teaching them. Those are things you probably see adults doing at your church, but Jesus didn't put an age requirement on this command. Although you are young, you are still invited and called to do important kingdom work.

In order to make disciples, we must go share the message of Jesus with those who need to know. You don't have to travel to foreign countries to go make disciples, but you may have to go outside of your comfort zone by starting a conversation with someone, which can lead to spiritual conversations. You can start at your lunch table, with your sports team, or the barista at your favorite coffee shop. No matter where you start, just remember that Jesus will be with you.

delight |

What does Jesus expect of us as we wait for His return?

How can you be part of the kingdom work He has given us as His followers to be doing?

display |

Jesus left us with a mission to accomplish. In the verses below, circle every command Jesus gives us in verses 19 through 20.

"Go, therefore, and make disciples of all nations, baptizing them

in the name of the Father and of the Son and of the Holy Spirit,

teaching them to observe everything I have commanded you. And

remember, I am with you always, to the end of the age."

As followers, we are called to "Go, make disciples, baptize, teach and remember." Jesus's mission was to seek and save the lost, and we are to complete the mission He gave us. How will you live out your mission today?

Acknowledge that Jesus has all authority in heaven and on earth and can be trusted. Thank Him for trusting you to carry out His mission. Ask for an increased desire to want to make disciples and for confidence to speak up about Him, silencing the voices of fear and doubt. Pray for the people all over the world that God will reach through your obedience to follow this command. Ask for a fresh reminder and awareness of His promise that He is with you until the end of the age.

FOR EVERY NAME, A NAIL

When you hear the word cross, what image flashes through your mind? A crosswalk, railroad crossties, an X, or even a "no crossing" sign? Or maybe you think first of Jesus, crucified on a wooden cross.

Whatever you might envision, the word cross always indicates an intersection; a change. In fact, Merriam-Webster defines a cross as a place of division, of choice, where we can move from one place to another, and even where our minds recognize truth—an "aha" moment of sorts.[1]

The cross of Jesus's crucifixion represented the intersection of what was and what would be:

- There, Jesus died for our past sins, but He also died for any sins we'd commit in the future.
- There, the old covenant of yearly sacrifice was replaced with the new covenant of Jesus's blood, poured out for us as the once-for-all-time sacrifice.
- There, the cross marked the final days of Jesus's earthly ministry and the beginning of ours.[2]

Maybe we could even say that the cross, those intersected beams, was the intersection of all of history itself. Each one of us stands in the middle of this intersection at some point, presented with a choice as we stand face-to-face with the image of a crucified Jesus: will I follow Him?

So, how did you meet Jesus in that intersection?

Maybe you've already walked through this intersection and said "yes" to Jesus. If so, think about what your life was like before the cross. To the left of the cross image on the next page, list a few words that describe your life before you knew Jesus. Then, on the right side of the cross image, list a few words that describe your life now, how Jesus has changed you.

Maybe you made a choice to follow your heart, to follow a friend, or to follow a movement, but you're here again in the intersection. Look at the cross image on this page. On the left side of the cross, list some words that describe how you felt about Jesus before beginning this devotional. On the right side of the cross, write out what you would choose now in the intersection.

In the Christian world, the cross has become almost synonymous with our faith. We see its image in church logos, on shirts, and even as jewelry pieces. So, maybe we've become numb to what it really represents. Today, as you think about the cross, remember Jesus. Remember that He was nailed to the cross. He was mocked and beaten and bloody. The one true and promised King emptied Himself of every right and privilege His position deserved to die to pay for the rebellion of His people and wash them in the grace of His blood.

Every name is written on a nail. We are all guilty here. But we all find Jesus here, too. We all find grace, forgiveness, freedom, hope, and a future here. Because of Jesus, our names are removed from the nails and written on the palms of His hands and in heaven (Isa. 49:16; Luke 10:20).

THREADS OF GRACE

Even after we face Jesus in the intersection of the cross, we may experience more intersections with the cross. Sometimes, we'll be faced with tough decisions, where we can choose to obey Jesus or go our own way; where Jesus said we have to "take up [our] cross daily" and choose to "follow [Him]" (Luke 9:23). And the truth is, sometimes we will make the wrong decision; we will choose not to follow Jesus; we will fail and fall short (see Rom. 3:23).

From the third chapter of Genesis, to the last page of the Bible, to our lives today, we see moments of failure woven throughout every story. But moments of failure—moments marked by sin—do not mark us as failures. Failure is a part of our story, but not a part of our identity. The beautiful truth of the gospel is that when you come to know Christ, you are not defined by what you've done, but what He has done for you. God is a loving and gracious Father who wants good things for His children—and that's who we are. When you look closely, you'll see threads of grace interwoven with every story of failure.

Close your eyes for a minute. Think about what you wrote around the cross in the article, "For Every Name, A Nail." Where do you see God's threads of grace? Write out a few examples along the thread on this page.

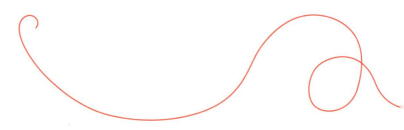

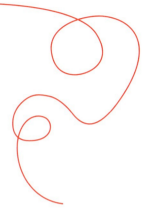

Now, review each moment of grace: find, write out, and speak aloud a scriptural truth that coincides with the grace threads in your story. Any time you feel like you've failed, repeat the process to remind yourself of what God says.

No matter how hard you chase after God and how much you want to pursue righteousness and godliness and not fail, sin will still be a part of your life. Jesus redeemed you, yes, but God promises to complete the good work He began in you (see Phil. 1:6). This means there's still room for you to grow. Even if you can't forget your mistakes, remember that you are forgiven. And God uses every part of your story, even your struggle, to draw you—and others—closer to Him.

END NOTES

1. "Cross Synonyms, Cross Antonyms," Merriam-Webster, accessed August 6, 2021, https://www.merriam-webster.com/thesaurus/cross.

2. Grant Osborne, "Cross, Crucifixion," in *Holman Illustrated Bible Dictionary*, ed. Trent C. Butler et al. (Nashville, TN: Holman Reference, 2003), pp. 368-371.